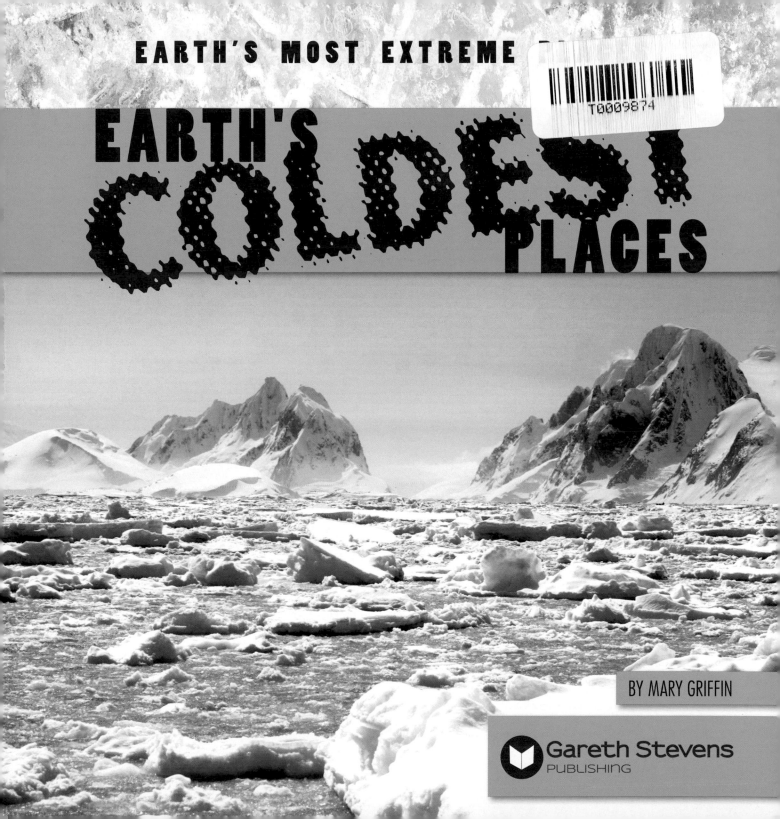

EARTH'S MOST EXTREME

EARTH'S COLDEST PLACES

T0009874

BY MARY GRIFFIN

Gareth Stevens
PUBLISHING

Please visit our website, www.garethstevens.com. For a free color catalog of all our high-quality books, call toll free 1-800-542-2595 or fax 1-877-542-2596.

Library of Congress Cataloging-in-Publication Data

Griffin, Mary, 1978- author.
Earth's coldest places / Mary Griffin.
pages cm. — (Earth's most extreme places)
Includes bibliographical references and index.
ISBN 978-1-4824-1890-3 (pbk.)
ISBN 978-1-4824-1889-7 (6 pack)
ISBN 978-1-4824-1891-0 (library binding)
1. Cold regions—Juvenile literature. 2. Extreme environments—Juvenile literature. 3. Climatology—Juvenile literature. 4. Polar regions—Juvenile literature. I. Title.
GB641.G78 2015
551.6—dc23

2014020525

First Edition

Published in 2015 by
Gareth Stevens Publishing
111 East 14th Street, Suite 349
New York, NY 10003

Copyright © 2015 Gareth Stevens Publishing

Designer: Katelyn E. Reynolds
Editor: Therese Shea

Photo credits: Cover, p. 1 Nataiki/Shutterstock.com; cover, pp. 1–24 (background texture) Serg Zastavkin/Shutterstock.com; p. 5 Volodymyr Goinyk/Shutterstock.com; p. 7 (Earth) NASA/GSFC/NOAA/USGS/Wikipedia.com; p. 7 (space background) Igor Kovalchuk/Shutterstock.com; p. 9 (photo) NOAA/Wikipedia.com; p. 9 (map) NASA/Wikipedia.com; p. 11 Gaelen Marsden/Wikipedia.com; p. 13 (map) Kennonv/Wikipedia.com; p. 13 (photo) Alexandra Kobalenko/All Canada Photos/Getty Images; p. 15 (map) AridOcean/Shutterstock.com; p. 15 (photo) George F. Mobley/National Geographic/Getty Images; p. 17 (map) Godruma/Shutterstock.com; p. 17 (photo) Amos Chapple/Lonely Planet Images/Getty Images; p. 19 Melissa McManus/The Image Bank/Getty Images; p. 21 Per Breiehagen/Time & Life Pictures/Getty Images.

Printed in the United States of America

CPSIA compliance information: Batch #CW15GS: For further information contact Gareth Stevens, New York, New York at 1-800-542-2595.

CONTENTS

Words in the glossary appear in **bold** type the first time they are used in the text.

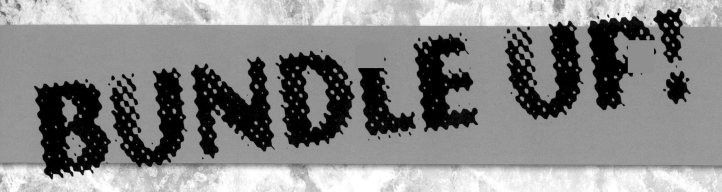

BUNDLE UP!

Do you like cold weather? Do you like getting bundled up to go sledding, skiing, or ice-skating? It gets cold enough in many parts of the world to freeze ponds and lakes. Some places get a lot of snowfall, too. For those who enjoy winter sports, this can be a lot of fun.

However, some places are so cold that not many living things can **survive** there—including people! Let's take a trip to some of the most interesting and incredibly cold places on Earth.

THAT'S EXTREME!

Earth's coldest temperatures occur about 60 miles (97 km) above the surface. Temperatures there can get as low as −146°F (−99°C).

4

Even though Antarctica is always very cold, many people visit to see its beautiful landscape.

WHY SO COLD?

Did you ever wonder why some places are hot, while others are cold? The imaginary line that goes around the middle of Earth is called the equator (ih-KWAY-tuhr). The sun points directly at places on the equator, so the sun's rays there are very hot. Places farther away from the equator are often cooler because the sun's rays hit at an angle.

Ocean currents are also responsible for temperatures. Some currents carry warm water to locations. That can make weather warmer there than at another place the same distance from the equator.

THAT'S EXTREME!

Ice and snow at the poles bounce some of the sun's rays back to space. That's another reason these places don't heat up.

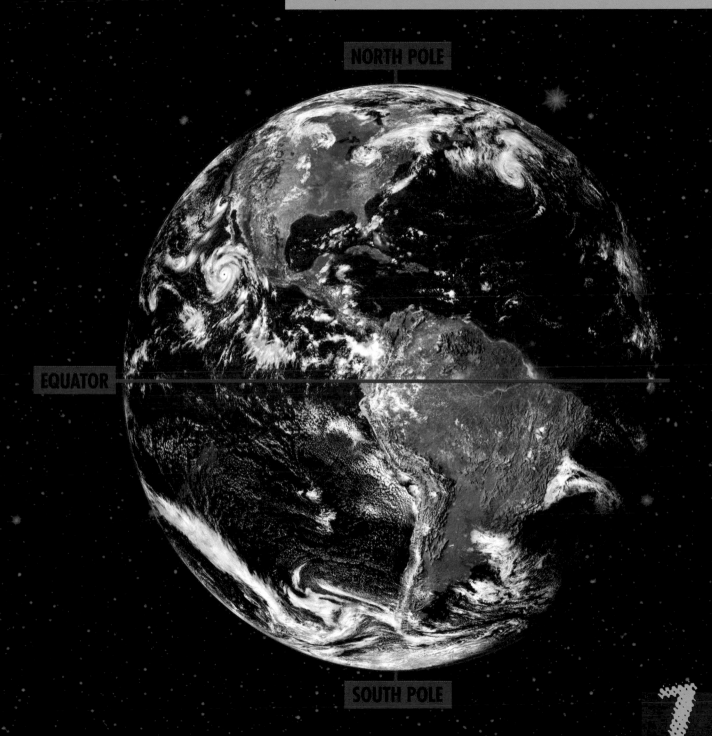

The equator is the same distance from the North and South Poles.

NORTH POLE

EQUATOR

SOUTH POLE

7

RECORD BREAKER

You might not be surprised to know Antarctica holds the record for coldest place on Earth. Scientists announced in December 2013 that they **recorded** a temperature of –135.8°F (–93.2°C) in eastern Antarctica. However, that temperature was actually set August 10, 2010! Instead of recording temperatures in person, scientists used **data** collected by several **satellites** over time to figure it out.

Before this record, the lowest temperature on Earth had been set in another place in Antarctica. Vostok Station, a **research** center, measured a temperature of –128.6°F (–89.2°C).

The coldest days in Antarctica are sunny days.
That's because clouds trap heat near Earth's surface.

Vostok Station

9

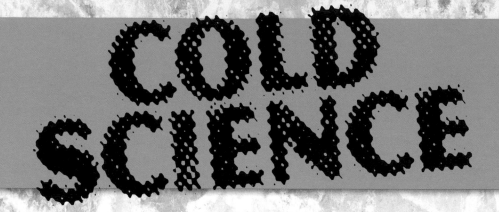

COLD SCIENCE

Temperatures in Antarctica are always very cold, way below freezing. Yet, some people do live there, mostly to do scientific research. Antarctica has more than 40 research stations. Many are made up of special buildings that are raised above the snow and ice.

When scientists travel outside to do work, they dress in several layers of special clothing. **Hypothermia** and **frostbite** are major concerns. Scientists may also need to put their tools in special cases so they don't freeze.

THAT'S EXTREME!

Because everything is frozen, research stations need special systems to melt snow for water supplies.

While about 1,000 people live at Antarctica's McMurdo Station in summer, only about 250 spend the winter there. It's operated by the United States.

MARS

There are also research stations in the Arctic, though the temperatures there aren't as low as Antarctica. The McGill Arctic Research Station (MARS) was founded in 1960 on Axel Heiberg Island in the Canadian Arctic. The **average** yearly temperature on Axel Heiberg Island is 5°F (–15°C).

Up to 12 people can stay at MARS to study glaciers, polar desert, and the kinds of life that can survive in such harsh locations. Scientists there also research **climate change** and its effect on the Arctic and the rest of the world.

THAT'S EXTREME!

Scientists have found living things in glaciers, which means that it's possible that life may exist on frozen planets.

This huge glacier is slowly flowing over Axel Heiberg Island.
Climate change means glaciers are melting and sea levels are rising.

Arctic Ocean

GREENLAND

Beaufort
Sea

AXEL HEIBERG ISLAND

Baffin
Bay

CANADA

Hudson
Bay

13

COLDEST US CITY

In the United States, the title of "coldest city" goes to Barrow, Alaska. In winter, the average low temperature is –20°F (–29°C). It's not much better in summer. The average over the entire year is only 11°F (–12°C).

This city of fewer than 5,000 people is also the northernmost US city. It's so far north that between late November and late January the sun doesn't rise. Another reason for Barrow's coldness is the wind coming off the Arctic Ocean.

THAT'S EXTREME!

Barrow can only be reached by plane or boat.

Native peoples make up half of the population of Barrow. Their ancestors have lived in this area for more than 1,000 years.

Barrow

ALASKA

15

A FROZEN CITY

A few cities claim the title "coldest city in the world." Many people give that honor to Yakutsk, Russia. The record low temperature in winter there is –81.4°F (–63°C). The average temperature in January is –34°F (–37°C). How cold is this? Many people don't wear their glasses outside because they can freeze to their skin!

However, more than 200,000 people live in Yakutsk. They dress in furs to keep warm, but rarely spend more than 20 minutes outdoors in the winter.

THAT'S EXTREME!

Despite the tough winter of Yakutsk, temperatures can raise as high as 90°F (32°C) in the summer!

When driving around Yakutsk in the winter, people usually don't turn off the engine in their car because they're afraid it'll freeze!

Yakutsk

FRIGID DENALI

Mount McKinley, or Denali, in Alaska is often thought to be the coldest mountain on Earth. Temperatures in the winter regularly dip below –40°F (–40°C). Some people have recorded even lower temperatures.

Denali is also North America's highest **peak** at 20,320 feet (6,194 m). That makes many mountain climbers want to get to the top—about 1,200 people a year. Strong winds and blinding snow often mean that climbers need to stop and pitch tents on their way up. Sadly, over 100 people have died trying to climb Denali.

THAT'S EXTREME!

Denali is one of the Seven Sisters. That's the name for a group of mountains made up of the highest mountain on each of the seven continents.

Denali is a Tanana Indian word that means "the high one."

19

ICEBOX OF THE NATION

Some people are proud to live in extremely cold places. Two US cities—International Falls, Minnesota, and Fraser, Colorado—went to court over which could call itself the "Icebox of the Nation." This meant it's the coldest city in the **continental** United States. International Falls won.

International Falls has an average yearly temperature of 37.8°F (3.2°C). It celebrates its cold weather with a 4-day **festival** called Icebox Days. People bowl with frozen turkeys, make snow figures, and ski by candlelight. No matter where people live, they try to make the best of their surroundings.

COLD WEATHER CONTEST: RECORD LOWS

International Falls, Minnesota: −55°F (−48°C)

Barrow, Alaska: −56°F (−49°C)

Axel Heiberg Island: −68.4°F (−55.8°C)

Denali: −75.5°F (−59.7°C)

Yakutsk, Russia: −81.4°F (−63°C)

Antarctica: −135.8°F (−93.2°C)

International Falls, Minnesota

21

GLOSSARY

average: a number that is figured out by adding numbers together and dividing the sum by the number of numbers

climate change: long-term change in Earth's climate, caused partly by human activities such as burning oil and natural gas

continental: being part of the United States that is made up of the lower 48 states. This excludes Alaska and Hawaii.

data: facts and figures

festival: a celebration

frostbite: a condition in which part of your body (such as your fingers or toes) freezes or almost freezes

hypothermia: dangerously low body temperature caused by cold conditions

peak: the pointed top of a mountain

record: to note officially. Also, to measure something.

research: studying to find something new

satellite: an object that circles Earth in order to collect and send information or aid in communication

survive: to live through something

FOR MORE INFORMATION

BOOKS

Besel, Jennifer M. *The Coldest Places on Earth*. Mankato, MN: Capstone Press, 2010.

Friedman, Mel. *Antarctica*. New York, NY: Children's Press, 2009.

Mack, Lorrie. *Arctic*. New York, NY: DK, 2007.

WEBSITES

Coldest Places on Earth
www.livescience.com/29913-coldest-places-on-earth.html
Read more about the places in this book and other frigid locations.

Ocean Currents and Climate
education.nationalgeographic.com/education/media/ocean-currents-and-climate/?ar_a=1
Watch a video about ocean currents and their effects on Earth.

INDEX

EARTH'S MOST EXTREME PLACES

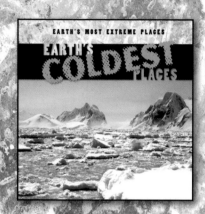

EARTH'S MOST EXTREME PLACES

EARTH'S
COLDEST PLACES

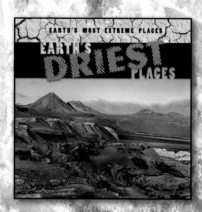

EARTH'S MOST EXTREME PLACES

EARTH'S
DRIEST PLACES

EARTH'S MOST EXTREME PLACES

EARTH'S
HIGHEST PLACES

EARTH'S MOST EXTREME PLACES

EARTH'S
HOTTEST PLACES

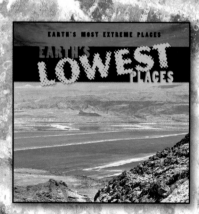

EARTH'S MOST EXTREME PLACES

EARTH'S
LOWEST PLACES

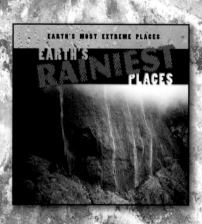

EARTH'S MOST EXTREME PLACES

EARTH'S
RAINIEST PLACES

Levels: GR: M; DRA: 28

ISBN: 978-1-4824-1890-3
6-pack ISBN: 978-1-4824-1889-7

9 781482 418903

Gareth Stevens
PUBLISHING